Lyrical Madness Entering Madness
A Book of Poetry

By
T. K. Pippin

PublishAmerica
Baltimore

First printing

At the specific preference of the author, PublishAmerica allowed this work to remain exactly as the author intended, verbatim, without editorial input.

ISBN: 1-4241-5149-X
PUBLISHED BY PUBLISHAMERICA, LLLP
www.publishamerica.com
Baltimore

Printed in the United States of America

Contents

Foreword

Before you begin your journey into madness, I would like to introduce myself and my work. My name is Tiffany K. Pippin. I grew up in the panhandle area of Florida (a.k.a. the Bible Belt of America). I was raised mostly by my mother, whom my brother and I lived with, after my parents' were separated in 1991 and later divorced.

I will start by saying I love both my parents, however, as most children go into the stages of adolescence, they start trying to form their own person, thereby rejecting or rearranging ideals instilled in them by their parents. This is also when the teenager starts to look back or remember things which might have happened to them growing up and analyzes scenarios. At least this is what happened with me.

We start to wonder what's on the other side when we die. What is true love and will I ever find it? Why have I forgotten some things or remembered others? Why am I so angry? Why won't they let me do this or that, or hang out with these kids or date this person or just be myself?

We start seeing contradictions in the teachings of our elders and start realizing we can surpass them. We understand that there are certain things you tell your parents, grandparents, teachers and pastors, and other things you tell your friends and your significant other. We are given experience, environment, and engagement from the outside world. We are to wear masks to conceal who we really are inside and we become miserable if we do not start to uncover the truth of ourselves and others, learning to love and forgive. Finding out that the universe and God is expandable and open for service. All we have to do is ask.

In this book you will travel through the mind of a child growing up and dealing with these questions, dealing with loneliness, learning about happiness, finding love and losing it, betrayal, death, drugs, spirituality and religion, trust, insanity, anger, friendship and the chaos that seems to con-fuse us. The poems are arranged neither in chronological nor categorical manner. Instead, they are arranged randomly so as to give variety to the eyes and mind, imitating the ups, downs and sideways of life.

Thank you, to all my family, friends and others who have inspired me on my life's journey. May you be blessed.

T. K. Pippin

Angry Adolescence

I saw my momma crying ‘cause she couldn’t pay the bills.
I saw my daddy lying and gambling on bad deals.
And now I’m ill because I only had one childhood;
Just one time to be innocent and young and now it’s gone.
I was sad as a kid and now I’m mad ‘cause you did
My lovely mother wrong. She was all alone with two kids,
While you were out with your drunken friends and
Coke-head slut girlfriend. I hated her and I hated you—
There wasn’t anything that I wouldn’t do to get back at you
For all the times I needed you to show me what a real man was,
So I wouldn’t have to go through all the hurt of bad relationships;
Boys who just used me, went through me, confused me
And threw me away like yesterday’s news.
No birthday presents or Christmas cards—no child support—
God it was hard to see so much dark.
I couldn’t take it. My heart kept breaking; the room kept
Shaking, and I felt completely naked.
Wearing hand-me-downs; the kids thought it was funny—
I wanted nicer things, so I saved up my lunch money.
God, it’s hard for a girl, living in this fucked-up crazy world.
And I don’t know if I would care if you died today.
I wouldn’t miss you ‘cause you were never there anyway.
Just give me some respect and listen to what I have to say to you.
Try to feel how I felt; it’s the least you can do.

2002

Bad Hand

Dropped into the lap of a mad mother—
Given to the hands of a hungry man.
Listening to the words of the worldly other—
Trying to break free but don't think she can.

The world is in a whirlwind
And dust has made you blind—
When everything is spinning,
Direction's hard to find.

Carrying her mind in a used syringe—
Looking into space that she's left behind.
Knowing what she's done would make you cringe—
Walking in her shoes would make you lose your mind.

The world is in a whirlwind,
You'll have to close your eyes—
It's hard to cling to truth,
When sifting through the lies.

Shedding second skin in a cheap motel—
Gazing past the face of an ugly man.
Needles carry heaven and this world has brought her hell—
She'll never see her future 'cause she's got a plan.

The world is in a whirlwind
And you're caught up in the show—
When every man has bought you,
It's all you'll ever know.

2003

Commotion

I will stimulate and perpetuate your mind
In a twisted and binding motion—
Creating thus a chaos
From such a great commotion.

Filling your brain to the rim
Just like a coffee cup.
Too much caffeine and a sugar high—
I've got you all wired up.

2001

Michelle Sinclair

Eighteen for just a day
And naked she lay,
On a pillow of black
And sheets of blood—
A potato in a sack,
Dumped in the mud.

Michelle, Michelle, what have you done?
You sought out the dark instead of the sun.
You sold your soul for money and fame;
You sold your body and shamed your name.
You're just another piece of meat—
A walking vagina out on the street.

Not enough alcohol to drown it down.
No happy places when he's going to town.
You're no longer a priceless catch.
You're no longer the beauty in the batch
Of cookies—you've been cut—
Cut like a slut!
          A slut!
           A slut!

You poor, unfortunate soul—
A porn star on a roll.
A smile to hide the pain;
A Lortab to hide the strain.
A Swiss cheese nose
White with cocaine.

You're already ruined; you're already bruised
You're diseased, rotten, unclean and used.

The snakes have been drawn to the pit—
On their prey they squeeze and spit.
The smell of flesh summons them;
Their victim meets a destiny grim.

2003

Long Live Loquacity

Long live loquacity—
For if it were not,
My rhymes would not be!

Long live loquacity—
That gives you to hear
And grants you to see!

Love live loquacity—
High telephone bills
And cable TV!

Long live loquacity—
Good speech, good reading,
Long letters to me!

Alas, long live loquacity—
That binds me to you,
And connects you to me.

2004

One-Sided Love

Flee back to your room;
Back to the dreadful tomb
You've made for yourself all these years.

After this fatal night,
You know you'll never invite
Into your heart another so welcomed guest.

He snatched your beating heart,
And you fell right from the start,
But sweet destiny would not take your side.

Your feelings and emotions he would astound,
When he dropped your heart to the ground,
And went off to find another.

1996

First Place in the Math Competition

Sometimes I feel like we're lifeless integers
In this complex mathematical equation.
We're added to the masses,
With reason being subtracted;
So our material things will multiply
And our hearts will be divided.
Trying to attain a higher percentage than the other,
Without a fraction to offer a starving brother.
Always wanting greater than what we have—
No one ever ends up being equal.

2003

Inside Out

Where's my skin?!
Where's my skin?!
It's rooted deep within.
The surface is tough—
Breaking through will be rough.

1995

Beaten

Will she find time
To break down the wall?

Will she find time
To uncover it all?

She can't drain the pain—
This kind of pain stains.

2000

Like Lead

Grandpa is dead;
Asleep in his bed.
J. Bird hangs his head—
Grief feels like lead.

Believe in a life
Without any strife—
But without any pain,
What joy do we gain?

Let go of the past,
'Cause we knew it wouldn't last.
Thought I'd found love in you,
But love thought you wouldn't do.

Baby I'm blue—
Blue without you.
High is the moon—
Tomorrow comes soon.

Believe in a life
Without any strife—
But without any pain,
What joy do we gain?

If the future holds my death,
Soon do I breathe my last breath?
Stones shaped like crosses;
Like old news life tosses-
Us aside.

2000

Taking a Trip

Blow up in my mind;
Side affects I might dread—
But just for tonight
I'm feeling alright.

Staring at this wall—
This wall is too tall.
Not even the king's
Horses and men
Could break my fall.

2000

Questions

Oh God, what is death,
That I might die as I speak?
I fear I cannot battle the demons
Inside me for I am too weak.

Will love pass by me one more time
And not stop to take a bite?
Will sweet heart turn to sour lime?
Will these emotions remain contrite?

2000

Stronger?

This is me—
Shredded by the claws of life;
Red and sticky,
Stuck in this hole
Dug by myself.

This is me—
Black and blue
From the blows
That fly from the mouths
Of those who know everything.

This is me—
Dirty and drab;
Scabbed from living
In mud holes with ground moles
And red-eyed demons.

This is me—
Plucked from the tree;
Spit from the mouth
Of the pretty bird
Who pierces my ears with his song.

And still, this is me—
Motionless, swollen, wet;
From the waters that swallowed me.
Alive, yes I survived;
If not to make me stronger…

Then why?

2003

Insight

To surrender to sadness is to die to depression;
But alas, I seek a new impression.

And leaving my thoughts behind,
I decline to speak out;
And resign to the safety of my bedroom.

But, my new feelings are reassured—
Only by reasons most absurd.

Then silence fills this space—
Where I recognize my Father's grace,
Falling upon my weary soul;
Filling this darkened hole,
That was dug by the world's false deities.

My direct outbursts, sometimes I'm told,
Are too forward, too harsh, and too bold.
But not enough as to be so cold
As their mocking has been on me.

They laughed at my Love,
And the Heavenly Dove that came from above-
To save their souls from a grim eternity.

In their own little heaven for now they'll be,
But in death, they'll have hell endlessly.

So I'll try over and over again,
To reach my worst foe and best friend—
For God!

1998

No One Else

No one else can move me to tears,
And no one else can remove all my fears
As You do.

No one else has power in his name,
And no one else can reach within me the same
As You do.

I'll read Your Word
And ponder Your Ways—
I'll drink You and You'll fill me,
Forever and always.

1998

My Wonderful Summer

Summer's voice speaks louder and louder—
Lawn mowers and sprinklers sing to each other.
Children on swing sets soaring through the air—
Their laughter makes me happy and I want to
Start swaying like the trees, waving to me in the breeze.
I'd climb up those trees and scrape my knees;
Remembering the times when childhood inhabited me—
Playing outside, riding bikes, flying kites.
Squirrels and birds dance to Nature's tune,
Bees tickle her flowers and new bud's bloom.
Warmth is the blanket of summer—
Diving into cool blue swimming pools,
Baking under the sun and learning about regret,
Licking melted candy bars from chocolate covered wrappers,
Running around the pool as hot pavement burns my feet,
Remnants of red icicle pops on my lips,
The smell of hotdogs and burgers sizzling on the grill,
Ice cream and snow cones chilling eager noses,
Sweet scents of flower blossoms and floating butterflies—
I can see it all right here in my mind's eye.
My shoulders and cheeks smudged from the sun's sweet kiss;
In the winter, my wonderful summer I miss.

2004

Wicked Wish

I'd like to kick in your head
And smash in your brain.
I'd like to bash in your skull
Again and again.

I'd like to cut off your fingers
And snip off your toes.
I'd like to scream in your ears
And bloody your nose.

I'd like to break your legs
And bust your knee caps.
Make you drink a laxative,
Then feed you your own crap.

Because you are full of shit,
And when you talk I can smell it.
The reason for this is as simple as can be;
You're a liar, a fake and repulsive to me.

2002

Faith

Who knows
Where Faith goes
When she walks out the door?
Can't find her anymore.

She said life feels
Like nothing's truly real—
Dreams lost with time,
Ambition lost its spine.

2002

One Thought

When children wake up to last night's morn,
Will they suffer the bruises of their father's scorn?

1999

Two Thoughts

This shiny blade seems so fair;
How could this friendly object scare?

Let me hold it in my grasp tonight,
To be my companion until the light.

1999

K.

She seems so sure of herself,
On the outside you'd never know
She's just her mother's daughter.
She's all grown up with two of her own,
But inside she's lost and all alone.
She's still a child but she can't see,
She moved just too fast to be
Her own person instead of being
Just her mother's daughter.
Bound by a circle of precious metal
To this man she does not love.
Crazy world produces too many like them—
The little girls will see right through them.
And what will she do,
When she finds that her pretty chicks are too,
Just their mother's daughters?

2003

Paper Tree

The world is falling down on me;
Too much hanging from my paper tree.

The light is dimming, I cannot see;
Too much hanging from my paper tree.

The clock is winding, it's almost three;
And there's too much hanging on my paper tree.

The room is spinning; I've lost my feet;
Too much hanging from my paper tree.

I had a dream last night at three;
In it, *I* was hanging from my paper tree.

It didn't kill me, fortunately;
It was too weak and couldn't support me.

Then the air started moving all around me;
The wind swept away my sweet paper tree.

2003

Betrayed by Thanksgiving

Time flies. Time flies.
Flies, screen doors, kitchens, pies—
Pumpkin pies and turkey breast,
Thanksgiving dinner—
Granny's best.
But it doesn't seem to matter to anyone.
Anyone can see
How distant we can be
When around family.
But I love them so;
So much that I couldn't bear
To tell the truth,
Because I'd be stripped bare—
Bare like her kitchen floor.
Bread to fry, milk to pour.
Poor me, poor me,
Pour me out and spill me;
Spilling my guts out to you.
Will you hear me?
Will you fear me?
I'm just a little too crazy,
And Pa Pa's just too lazy,
To have made a good husband
For this silver-headed woman.
Needs motivation, concentration, dedication—
But alienation is all that's received.
And we're betrayed by another Thanksgiving dinner.

2001

Indifference to You

I don't care who you've made,
And I don't care who you've saved.
I don't care who's dying now;
I don't care if you're crying now—
'Cause I made you my bliss,
And I gave you my kiss,
But you gave me your shit.

I don't care what you're thinking—
I've sailed on that boat
But jumped as it was sinking.
My new indifference to you
Should give you a clue
That I won't take your shit.

2002

Fish Tank

I took a look into a glassy fish tank;
I drowned myself and watched how I sank.

My brown eyes into the wet air they did stare;
A most unlively, a most deathly glare.

My stiff limbs made no motion at all,
Except when shifted by the water cushioning my fall.

My skin was no longer peachy-rose true,
But new shades of color such as purple and blue.

Bouncing lifelessly on the fish tank floor,
To face your sarcasm and cynicism no more.

1997

Skirt

She's a Madame Butterfly,
She's so pretty.
She's got all the little boys
Wrapped in her wings.
So when the party's over and done,
And all the girls have gone but one,
She'll stay and play
With the boys and have some fun.

'Cause she's the skirt
That never played well with the girls.
She's got rosy cheeks, red lips
And caramel curls.
Well she's got a nasty bite you know,
But the boys can't see past her bright glow,
So they'll stay, and play
Until the ending of her show.

2002

My Roses

My roses are red
But they won't bloom—
Because darkness has come
And I've met my doom.

1995

Season of Shooting

Has safety left our vocabulary?
Will fear become us all?
Bullets will cease the interest in learning—
And the children from playing ball.

The sounds of blasts have burst our ears
As shots ring through the halls!
Oh God, is there a haven here?
Must we hide in bathroom stalls?

The screams have become numb to my ears,
And footsteps are all I hear.
Closer and closer and closer to me—
They're getting nearer I fear!

I cannot breathe,
I cannot cry—
For noise I fear
Will cause me to die.

Have I ever prayed as hard as now?
Does blood drip like sweat from my brow?
Will Jesus remember me and let me in,
After the slaughter of the cow?

2002

Run Away-Maybe Stay

Not exactly the perfect son or daughter?
Aren't living up to your parents' dreams?
This living up is just too much!
Our mouths release loud shrill screams.

My life is theirs and not my own—
Does this mean I should leave my home?
Leave behind all my prized possessions—
Follow my dreams and capture obsessions?

Should I deny my up-bringing,
And make for myself a new life?
Give up my morals and child-like thoughts—
Bring unto my living being strife?

So, I'll stay here in my room—
Confined momentarily for a minor crime.
Instead of running from my feelings,
I'll sit and meditate on their sweet sublime.

1995

Just Me

No one else is haunted by your face—
Your laugh, your past, your awkward embrace—
Just me.

1998

My Lord

When opened, my eyes are blind.
When closed and focused
The picture becomes clear—
How divine my Lord really is.
His word guides me.
His strength empowers me.
Her mystery enchants me.
His wrath humbles me.
His power amazes me.
Her gentleness embraces me.
His might thrills me.
His love is given to me.
His death saves me.
Her life renews me,
After my sins kill me.
He is alive in me.
She leads me through darkness.
She calls to me when I am searching.
His crucifixion saddens me.
His resurrection gladdens me.
The very thought of how wonderfully beautiful,
Omnipotent, merciful and gracious my God is,
Sends chills down my spine.
She is all I live for,
And all I will die for.
He is who I will spend eternity with—
He is She, my Source, my Lord.

1997

Tidbit

Insanity swimming around in my head—
Control hangs on by one tiny thread.

1999

Letter

To the ones with shattered hearts
Who gave the one hundred and all
And never got but the none
Our passion will never run out
And the world will suffer great loss
When our lives have moved on to their treasure
The songs of life will be sung
Through the wavy grass fields
And bees will taste it on their tongues
When sweet nectar pleases it
The sky is our roof
Trees and mountains our walls
Which build our homes around us
There are no limits to our thoughts
And our hearts will beat forever

To the ones whose souls
Are deeper than the deepest black nothing
And to look into their eyes
One could see the universe
These are the ones I could not compete with
Their truth always overcame my surface
And I will forever be grateful
To the ones who could look past the ugly

2002

Deep Within My Mind

You'll never know the words that pass through me—
The poetry and rhymes that I often see.
Everything I do, my mind creates inside—
New stories and pictures, many of which I hide…

Deep within my mind.

You'll never see the beauty I hold within,
The passionate flame that grows beneath my skin—
That will one day carry me away to that place
That waits for me in another space…

Deep within my mind.

Can I share with you my thoughts and finds?
Blessed be the tie that binds—
Our souls together with fervent heat,
That feeds our hearts and makes them beat…

Deep within my mind.

1998

Green

Green like you, little brother
Was the sack you held in your hand

Without it you were a fireball
Mean like the dusty wind

But as its smoke filled
Your asthmatic lungs

You'd sit like a Native 'round a bonfire
And I joined in on the ceremony

Toke, toke, toking on your hand-made pipe
An expert on your shop-class special

You were three years my junior
Yet more experienced than me

Dirt under your fingernails
From breaking down the bud

Rolling perfect cylinders
Round and fat like fingers

You wouldn't be broke from buying the bowl
Because you could still sling it swiftly

And bags would fly from your hands
Into the lungs of your friends

Sweet smell of sticky and shake
Smoke shimmies its way to my nose

We talked, predicted, and became philosophers
Da Vincis and Ecshers in our own world

The fighting would cease between us
And peace came at those moments

We knew we loved each other
Though our words were sometimes harsh

This is my apple pie in life
These are the days I'll never forget

When we're old we'll look back on these times
When we were in the green of our lives

2000

A Tree's Tale

Smoking under the starry darkness
On a moonlit carpet of green,
Gazing onto a pond of glass,
Reflections of other world's unseen.
Conversing over candlelight
And tightly twisted twigs.
Traces of skinny smoke stacks
Singing snake-like songs and jigs.

2004

Me, My Twin

We used the paddle boat.
We paddled out to the
Middle of the lake,
Me and Tiffany.

As we admired the late
Afternoon, peace shed
Over the water and she
Stared into the distance.

She asked me,
"Have you ever wished
You could just float
Away forever?"

I just looked at her with
A half-grin, reflecting.
She glanced at me briefly,
But with more to say.

I could see it in her eyes
Then she looked away.
I wanted to hold her and
Just before I could answer

She yelled, "Let's swim!"
She jumped in.
"Come on," she urged.
I dove in after her.

Contradiction

I am the death that lives.
I am the child that is grown.
I am the darkness that walks in light
I am the man inside the woman.
I am the depression clothed with delight.
I am the disease that never dies.
I am the tears felt deep inside the dry.
I am the screams behind the laughs.
I am the hurt that's never healed.
I am the hate that was hurt by love.
I am the crow that wants to be a dove.
I am the misdirection guided by good time.
I am an honest contradiction.

2003

Manifestation

She stares at her dark curtains
As she lies in her bed.
So much dismay and confusion
Spinning around in her head.

She wondered for hours about
The words defending me and you
"Father, please forgive them,
For they know not what they do."

Her tears kissed her pillow,
As she thought of things she'd done.
How could You love someone so filthy?
So much to sacrifice Your only Son?

Virgin lacking virginity;
Clean turned into soiled.
Thoughts were twisted in her mind,
Like her hair was curly and coiled.

Her life is not all roses,
But in her garden flowers grow.
How does she get through her troubles?
It's knowing, when she dies, where she'll go.

She knows that Christ is alive.
He's living in you and in me.
What is her purpose in life?
It's helping the blind to see.

1997

Search

Lost treasures are found
At the bottom of the sea—
Never to be discovered.
Until reached within me.

1995

Rolling and Unrolling

Don't deal—
But I know this pill
Will fuck you up.

Don't deal—
But I feel this pill
Is fucking me up.

Senses enhanced—
He'll want to get
Into my pants.

I'll give him a dance—
But he won't get
Into these pants.

Don't deal—
But I just might be
In love with this pill.

2001

Leave Me Wanting

I just wanted an object to crave;
With someone else to misbehave.
Was it you I fell in love with, or that strong emotion?
I just wanted to swim in your ocean.

When your lips met mine
Our feelings did intertwine.
There is much more than this,
But it's started with a kiss.

I wanted so much more,
But you were scared to open the door.
Do you think of me, or am I the only one troubled?
Thoughts of your strong embraces are doubled.

My body feels numb; it cannot attest
To the many emotions swelling deep in my chest.
Do you gaze at me or just glance and walk away?
Please come hold me and say you'll stay.

I felt at home when you held me in your arms.
I gave in to your eyes, your touch, your charm.
Why can't I seem to get through this pain?
Wondering if you'll ever hold me again.

1996

Short Flight

Sometimes I'm sure that I could die,
But most times I wish that I could fly—
Off to a foreign land,
Where I'd hold my lover's hand.

But I feel that my wings are broken,
That I was pawned for some small token—
Kept in my cage surrounded by bars,
Set by the window to watch passing cars.

1995

Unclean

The child has died.
The soul has diminished.
Depression seeps through
The veins, pumping life
Back into the child.
Back to a life filled
With anguish and hatred;
Full of demons and personalities.
Heart of black stone
Made me hard and cold—
God's child made unclean
By stories left untold.
Thoughts rolling through
A young child's head—
Don't hurt me.
Don't tell.
Someone help me; I need help!
Why couldn't I say no?
Am I unclean now?
If so, then how?
Shame overflows in me,
And I'm twisted inside.
I'm not the same,
But too different to explain.
What happened to the cheerfulness
And the innocent joy inside?
Has it gone away forever to hide?
Now, I am unclean.

1994

The Way It Should Be

Happy children,
A mother and father,
Married and in love.
One house; one home—
This is the way it should be.

Now the children are sad.
Two angry, different parents,
Divided and in war.
Two houses; no home.
This is not the way it should be.

Tearing the hearts of one another—
Trying to find a solution
To a problem that was
Caused by themselves.
I can't believe this is how it should be.

Throughout the children's minds
Hatred is spread.
Their poor hearts are misled—
Learning to fight instead
Of loving and trusting others.
You decide the way it should be.

1995

Death

When there's nothing but silence,
And you're searching your mind;
You can't get out of bed,
And your teeth start to grind.

When your life isn't worth living,
And you can't stand the pain;
You're down really low,
And you lose, never gain.

Suicide comes to mind.
But it doesn't work out right—
So you have to try again,
After you've lost the fight.

Now you can't think;
You can't hear a thing.
Finally you see the light—
You can hear the bells ring.

But it's not bells you hear—
Oh no, dear friend, it's not.
That's the sound of chains,
On hell's demons that sit and rot.

You wonder if this is it,
What you've wasted your life for—
Now you've found out,
There's more pain than before.

1996

Spring

Spring kisses my senses with
Orange, yellow, red and purple-
Speckled highways filled with dreams.

So green and full are the trees
With hints of yellow like highlights
From the sun on a baby's head.

Bright blue sky so far, so high,
Freckled by cotton ball clouds,
Pregnant with expectant rains.

Spring kisses my senses with
Silver-blue waters like mirrors
Reflecting radiant images of creation.

White splashes from waving arms
Bring smiles to friends' faces,
Filling them with laughter and delight.

There is a certain joyfulness
In knowing that in Spring,
All the pretty flowers bloom
And all the birds will sing.

In the Future

In years of old…

We will reminisce about smoke rings and resonated fingers, flicking ashes into foam cups filled with water, wasting our time talking amongst ourselves about what we'll look like twenty years from now…

Wishing we were young again.

2004

Not Wanting

This is my telephone
It's big, yellow, about 20 years old
With an insert for a telephone book
It rings
But I don't want to answer it

This is my Mello Yello
The color of a flower stem
It rises like a rocket to my lips
Cool and refreshing
But I don't want to swallow it

This is my computer
An HP Pavilion
Interesting, entertaining, educational
Packed with information
But I don't want to turn it on

This is my halter top
Black, strappy and sexy
Pleasing to the eye
An automatic boy magnet
But I don't want to put it on

This is my October fling
Gorgeous, blue eyes, gelled hair
With blonde highlighted tips
Baggy jeans and a visor
But I don't want to see him

This is the door to my fate
The insight to unanswered questions
A light at the end of the tunnel
A glimpse into eternity
But I don't want to cross the threshold

2000

Treasures

Heirlooms are kept
In boxes and treasured;
But the price of great things
Is not to be measured.

1996

Drained

Water trickling down the drain,
Pours into my wicked brain.

Must I know what's in the hole,
To control what seeps into my soul?

How can I smile, how can I frown,
When nothingness is all that's around?

Please magic don't let my feet touch the floor.
Please abstinence don't give me into the score.

Leave me tonight with a pen and some wine,
And tomorrow everything will seem just fine.

1997

You Laughed When You Left

Your hair was soft like sand in my hands—
Sand from the beaches in the Gulf of Mexico.
Soft like the hair on a baby's head—
And I babied you, I mothered you,
I ruined it all and smothered you.

Your eyes were like the ocean, full of life—
Like the waters that swallow the Bahamas.
Blue-green like the crayon I held in my hand,
Controlling each mark you made—
But you couldn't stay in the lines.

You stayed until the day the oak tree cried
From your cuts through its heart and our names—
Like a paper-cut underneath my fingernail,
The kind you can't reach, that knags and
Laughs at you. You laughed when you left.

2000

The Prize

It seems confusion is in the air,
When we can look into space and stare
At billions of hard-earned dollars spent
On contraptions that have never meant
Anything to our starving bellies.

We've got our flag planted in dirt,
But our own weak and diseased still hurt.
Having no budget for healthcare and cures,
This misplacement of tax money stirs
In my heart an angry tornado.

I wonder when I look at the moon
If my big break will be coming soon.
While NASA sent millions to Mars,
I was broke and wishing on stars
That one day I'd crawl out of this hole.

Will America ever get out of debt?
Will our Social Security budget be met?
Why do we send people to space,
When we can't repair our own home place?
Our government's chasing the prize.

2004

Escape

"A conscious effort to forget reality and mental troubles by taking up some other powerful interest."-Webster's Dictionary.

Reality stomps me into the ground.
Will fantasy and escape ever come around?
My dreams die a little more every day—
I'm not content with living your way.

Something smooth lies under the bark.
The light is bright, but concealed by the dark.
Digging hard for truth, my fingers are rubbed raw—
So my truth won't be found, I'll cover up my flaw.

Can utopia be achieved only by death?
If so, tonight I will breathe my last breath.
The world will burn and fade away—
And heaven will be love's hide-away.

1997

Best Friends Forever

You are my best friend
I'll be with you until the end

I won't leave you
I won't deceive you
I'll try to believe you
But I'll never leave you

You are my best friend
We'll live life hand-in-hand

I will give to you
I will live for you

But don't leave me
I'll turn, believe me
You can't deceive me
I'll turn, believe me

You don't want me as your enemy

The Fairest

There was once a castle
High upon a mountain—
Where a fair princess resided
And drank from a youthful fountain.

She had seven maidens
Which doted and pampered her.
They'd make her cinnamon toast;
Her coffee and cream they'd stir

Her dresses were made of silk,
With satin, chiffon and lace.
Her hair was gold and glimmered—
Pure beauty enveloped her face.

But one day as she woke up
And her maidens helped her from bed,
She noticed her legs weren't working
And things were spinning inside her head.

Her hands began to shake
And her stomach felt like lead—
She started crying hysterically,
And then she fell down dead.

There was once a little shack
At the base of the mountain high,
Where lived a poor little maiden
Who wanted to touch the sky.

She found her place in the castle
As a maiden to the princess fair.
She was jealous of her beauty;
Her purity she could not bare.

One morning she fixed her coffee—
A tainted sort of brew.
And so the princess fell over;
The maiden's job was through.

Doll

What do I have but a doll's face,
Painted pretty for presentation?
Lipstick and powder won't last forever,
But for the moment they'll hide the pain.

Held back tears mistaken for glassy eyes—
They're brown and beautiful with mascara
And eye shadow. Posing interest, but they
Stare past the diversion into the memories
That want to be forgotten.

Suck it in; don't let them see the sweets.
Run it off the next day; it will be all right.
Playing dress-up is getting old—
Too many surface stories being told.

My beauty sleep can conjure ugly nightmares,
But my few sweet dreams I treasure:
Embraced by a bounty of blankets—
Quickly covered up to keep out the cold.

Orange-Banana-Oddball

What is this orange-banana-oddball?
Jumping from buildings and surviving the fall?

My Indian spirit's locked inside—
Afraid to reveal this wild that I hide.

I know that I'm different, and insanely strange—
Some of these thoughts I try to arrange.

I'll sit still, as still as death—
I'll punch my pillow and hold my breath.

This orange-banana-oddball am I—
This banana peel slip, bleed and die.

1998

Deceased Unknown

I'm in my Sunday's best floral dress,
Hair pulled half-way up and looking like a doll.
We're going to meet Granny and Pa Pa
So we can all ride together in one car.
Granny's house always has that same smell—
Cornbread and dressing hot from the oven.
She's cooked something today too,
But it's hidden under a tinfoil covered dish.
Paige, my favorite cousin to play with,
Is riding with us to the church too.
She's got red hair, she's pale and funny,
But today she looks sad and is quiet—
It's awkward with all the silence,
Like a squiggly worm dug up from the earth.
On the way to the church, Pa Pa drives
By *the* house. The skeleton of this once
Three bedroom, two bath, brick home
Still has smoke streams rising from its ashes.
They put the fire out at 4:23 a.m. yesterday.
I can see a stove unit, *the* stove unit, and what
Used to be a bed. Was it her bed?
There's a dog rummaging through all the piles
Of years. The drive seems so far away as we pass
By oaks and wheat, the pines and hay—
Green and gold flashes by my eyes.
The church is as white as a cloud, inside and out.
The pews inside are dark brown like Dark
Chocolate Hershey's candy bars. It smells like
Flowers, even more so at the front of the church
Where bouquets of colors and condolences congregate.
It's so bright and sunny outside—
I love the way light beams through stained glass.

I squint my eyes. I should be outside, riding a
Four-wheeler or jumping on the trampoline!
Mom always said that if she and Dad died
That Chris and I could go live with either
Granddaddy or Uncle Clayton. I'd choose
Granddaddy because Clayton's kids are rude
And spoiled—and I don't want to end up like that.
Everyone is crying but me and the babies.
Their faces are all wet and red blotched.
I feel like a white hair on an eight-year-olds' head.
How can I cry when I don't even know them?

Grief's Drill

They say time heals
But Bill won't believe,
'Cause he remembers the day
That his daddy did leave.
Packed up and left
His family on the shelf;
Went off to make
A new life for himself.
On holidays he saw him
With his new wife to be—
Sweet sixteen years
Younger than he.
I frequently ask Bill
If he'll ever change his mind—
He says these father-son things
Rarely work out; good fathers
Are too hard to find.
Boy, you know the drill
And I know it too,
But I remember the time
I loved a boy like you.
Your heart's stone cold,
Frozen by time
Lemon-lime inside from
Your daddy's past crime.
Sometimes with life it's hard to deal.
Come on boy, you know the drill.

Boredom

Boredom is ringing in my ears;
Boredom is ringing in my fears!
Screaming inside my beating heart;
Tearing my silk soft skin apart!

Boredom is ringing in my ears;
Boredom is streaming in my tears!
I cannot take much more of this pain!
Who are you to tell me I'm insane?

One day I'll be the lucky one—
One day my freedom will finally come.

We all want the glamour.
We'd all like the fame.
Our outsides are different,
But inside we are the same.

1996

Mrs. Patty

Mrs. Patty smiles.
When others frown,
It won't pull her down—
All the while,
Mrs. Patty will smile.

She says she loves Jesus,
And I can tell
He loves her—
Because of her smile.

Mrs. Patty smiles.
When others frown,
It won't pull her down—
All the while,
Mrs. Patty will smile.

She'll sing out loud,
Though not the best.
But she'll praise him
Regardless of all the rest.

Mrs. Patty smiles.
When others frown,
It won't pull her down—
All the while,
Mrs. Patty will smile.

Some of the purest joy,
She'll hold like a favorite toy.
But it really holds her—
I can tell by her smile.

Mrs. Patty smiles.
When others frown,
It won't pull her down—
All the while,
Mrs. Patty will smile.

Through the rough
She smiles bold.
Through the heat, rain and cold,
She knows He's in control.

Mrs. Patty smiles.
When others frown,
It won't drag her down—
All the while,
Mrs. Patty will smile.

And one day when all is gone
But a chosen few and the Holy One,
The Father will look down on
Mrs. Patty and smile.

Floating

Wind, wind, blow me away,
Or my sorrows will drive me mad.
Time, time, how long is the day,
That makes me so lonely and sad?

Dreams, dreams, my realities bend
And draw me back into my mind.
Moon, moon, will you be my friend,
And stop all the faces that wind?

Birds, birds, sing happy songs,
That please my soft, rounded ears.
My heart, my heart, oh how it longs,
But is captured by all of its fears.

Shoes, shoes, carry my feet
To the water of which I have thirst.
My love, my love, your spirit is so sweet,
That joy inside me would burst!

1997

Fat Woman in the Pharmacy

Good God, woman!

Have I ever seen such a fat person still walking?
Pound for pound pounding against the purple
And white tile floor and onto the gray carpet.

And I wonder, does it feel the pain
Of each darkened imprint; the years of
Too many Twinkies and TV dinners?

All this stuffed into your big-n-tall turquoise pants.
It reminds me of the sea, waves of cellulite
Rolling in sequence. Or of green-colored

Hills in a Bob Ross painting—happy hills
And happy trees. Tree trunk legs,
Thick and heavy; hard to move.

How hard it must be to find clothes to fit
Such a large mass. I wonder, how many
Richard Simmons motivational tapes do you own,

Metabolite pills have you swallowed,
Protein power plans have you purchased, Billy
Blank Videos have you bought?

Has your couch made a permanent parking space
For you? Your pretty face with pouty lips
Takes pride in its jaw muscles.

Even though I know it's your own fault
For not fasting, I also pity you because I would
Never want to see that figure in my mirror—

Fat woman in the pharmacy.

2000

Perseverance

Scream, so the world can hear.
Shout your opinions even though
They say your words don't matter.

I will make my voice be heard
Through the thick chaos.
My beliefs I'll make known—
You'll feel them pass through you.

You cannot stop me;
You cannot silence me,
Because by law I'm free—
Free so my spirit forever will be.

Death does not frighten me,
It only encourages me.
Fear cannot grasp me;
It only pushes me closer to my cause.

Our determination will impress you;
Your condition will distress you.
One day you will be broken—
Blood has bought your token.

Twisted Thoughts

Oh, how joyful, the twisted thoughts
That control my weakened mind.
To think of things that seem insane—
Does this make me myself insane?
I should tell you of this so you could know.
Don't think of me as a sick lunatic
When I tell you my stories of hallucinations—
Of poking your skin with a thousand needles;
Cutting off all your hair while you sleep,
Then laughing at you when you wake—
Dancing to the beautiful music of a boys' choir
With the deceased members of your family.
Are chills running down your spine yet?
After your humiliation with your course,
Shagged, pitiful mop of hair
I dismember you while you're still alive;
Screaming for someone to save you,
But no one listens to you,
Because they hate you, as do I.
And they follow me, and help me,
Because they love me;
Do anything for me.
After I cut off your limbs,
I burn the ends, so you will not bleed to death—
More torture is yet to come.

1996

Porn Stars and Pork Skins

Porn stars and pork skins
Are not that different I think—
Because porn stars and pork skins
Both go good with a drink.

Porn stars and pork skins
Are both edible you see?
And porn stars and pork skins
Are both neither costly nor free.

Porn stars and pork skins
Both require coke on the side.
And porn stars and pork skins
Are both fake new world lies.

Porn stars and pork skins
Can both be good to taste.
But porn stars and pork skins
Bring big regret in haste.

Porn stars and pork skins
Are not healthy and fresh—
Porn stars and pork skins
Are just dead, dried up flesh.

Porn stars and pork skins
Are of low-grade quality—
Because porn stars and pork skins
Are sold in quantity.

Porn stars and pork skins
Both suck a fat dick.
And porn stars and pork skins
Make me fucking sick.

2004

This Man

This man who learned to love life
Yet felt trapped by his own dying body.
This man did not fear his death
But the progression taking him there.

This man who knew the answers to mysteries
But could not heal his own disease.
This man who knew the secrets of life
Yet his own slipped through his hands.

His name is not important,
His body is no longer here,
His impression was made forever
In hearts who held him dear.

Closing the Curtain

I'm closing the curtain now;
I'm putting up my steel.
I'm forgiving what used to
Grip me so tight;
It's time for me to heal.

But I cannot move forward,
Until I right what was wrong;
Until I acknowledge the
Sorrow and loss and shame
For not being strong.

There once was a joy deep
Inside me—
It shown when I was a child.
It gave me a magnetic energy,
But ambivalence has made it mild.

You entered what was
Forbidden;
You lead God's child to sin.
You brought me into this cage
You created,
And then you locked me in

For years and years I've
Screamed and cried;
Mad as hell and full of pride.
Waiting to take revenge on you;
Thrown on the altar,
Snatched from the pew.

But I cannot move forward,
Until I right what was wrong;
Until I acknowledge the
Sorrow and loss and shame
For not being strong.

I'm closing the curtain now;
I'm putting up my steel.
I'm forgiving what used to
Grip me so tight;
It's time for me to heal.

Printed in the United States
74627LV00004B/585

9 781424 151493